# Everything You Need to Know About

# ADD/ADHD

ADD/ADHD is a medical disorder that causes daydreaming, forgetfulness, hyperactivity, and other problems.

Everything You Need to Know About

# ADD/ADHD

Eileen Beal

THE ROSEN PUBLISHING GROUP, INC.
NEW YORK

Published in 1998 by The Rosen Publishing Group, Inc.
29 East 21st Street, New York, NY 10010

First Edition
Copyright © 1998 by The Rosen Publishing Group, Inc.

**Library of Congress Cataloging-in-Publication Data**

Beal, Eileen.
 Everything you need to know about ADD/ADHD / Eileen Beal.
 p.    cm. -- (The need to know library)
 Includes bibliographical references and index.
 Summary: Defines both attention deficit disorder and attention deficit
hyperactivity disorder and discusses what can be done to treat these conditions, including medication, behavior modification, and counseling.
   ISBN 0-8239-2748-2
   1. Attention deficit hyperactivity disorder—Juvenile literature.
[1. Attention deficit hyperactivity disorder.] I. Title. II. Series.
RJ506.H9B42 1998
616.85'89—dc21                                             97-45149
                                                              CIP
                                                              AC

*Manufactured in the United States of America*

# Contents

# Introduction:
## A Day in the Life

*A*t home, Annette can never find things in her room, and she's always forgetting things—her purse, dates with her boyfriend, where she left the family car. She gets along well with her parents, though they are always on her case about her forgetfulness, laziness, and poor grades.

In school, Annette is barely making it. Her teachers complain about her daydreaming and forgetfulness. She always shows up in class without homework or books, no matter how hard she tries. She can't make herself pay attention in class, either.

Though she'll never admit it, Annette doesn't always understand her teachers when they explain things, especially directions for classwork and tests. She seldom turns in a completed classwork assignment and she never finishes a test before the bell rings. Annette's classmates like her, but that doesn't stop them from teasing.

*Juan is a human hurricane. At home, his room is a disaster area, and he's always breaking things—juice bottles, backdoor windows, his arms. Hardly a day goes by that he doesn't blow up at his brothers or get into an argument with his mother.*

*At school, things are worse. His locker is hopelessly messy. In class, except gym, which he loves, he's either zoning out or acting up. He seldom does classwork because he can't remember to bring supplies, and he has given up totally on homework. At lunchtime he shoves and pushes in the cafeteria line, and he usually ends up eating alone. He's in detention at least once a week.*

Annette isn't a ditsy daydreamer—she has a moderate case of Attention Deficit Disorder (ADD). Juan isn't a dummy or bully—he has a severe case of Attention Deficit Hyperactivity Disorder (ADHD). That means he has the same problem Annette has, and he is also extremely impulsive and overactive.

ADD and ADHD are disorders that are diagnosed more and more frequently in teens. And if your life is like Annette's or Juan's, it's possible that you may have ADD or ADHD too.

This book will give you the facts about ADD and ADHD: what they are, where they come from, and how to manage them. You may be surprised to know that ADD and ADHD are common and treatable. And they may give you special talents and gifts that you didn't know you had.

People with ADD/ADHD usually have organizational problems
and are impatient.

# Chapter 1

# What is ADD/ADHD?

ADD and ADHD are often grouped together and thought of as ADD/ADHD. Both are medical, not behavior, disorders. There are differences between them.

ADD, or attention deficit disorder, causes people to be inattentive and easily distracted. With ADHD, or attention deficit hyperactivity disorder, people have the qualities of ADD but also are impulsive or hyperactive.

Medical scientists think that ADD and ADHD are caused by a chemical problem in the brain. The front part of the brain (right behind the forehead) helps you pay attention, concentrate, organize things, and put the brakes on impulsive or unacceptable behavior. In people with ADD or ADHD, the front part of the brain may not be able to use the brain's main signal senders, neurotransmitters, the way it is supposed to.

The front part of the brain has very little to do with intelligence, so it is possible to be very smart and still have ADD or ADHD.

## Who Gets ADD/ADHD?

Three to five percent of school-age children are affected by ADD or ADHD. That means that out of every 100 people in your school, three to five of them are affected to some degree by ADD or ADHD.

More boys are diagnosed with ADD/ADHD than are girls. This may be for a reason. Hyperactivity is easy to spot, and more boys than girls tend to be hyperactive. For people who are not hyperactive, their ADD/ADHD can go undiagnosed for many years (in some cases, a lifetime).

Medical research has shown that there is a definite genetic link behind ADD/ADHD. So if one person in a family has ADD or ADHD, there is a very good chance that someone else in the family had or has it, too.

## How Is ADD/ADHD Diagnosed?

It is best to get evaluated for ADD or ADHD as early as possible. In most cases, someone at school—a teacher, counselor, or principal—suggests that a student be tested or evaluated for ADD/ADHD. Evaluations do not take much time, and they are usually done in two parts.

First, a student takes one or more of the following tests:
- Intelligence—to help evaluate the student's IQ and reasoning abilities

One way to evaluate a person for ADD/ADHD is to administer a series of tests.

- Achievement—to find the actual grade level the student is working at
- Fine motor skills—to see if there are problems with the student's hand-eye coordination and/or writing skills

Then the student is evaluated (tested, examined, reported on, observed) by two or more of the following "experts":

- Parents—are asked to describe their child's behavior over a long period of time
- Teachers—are asked to rate the student's behavior using standardized forms, and to give their personal opinion of the student's school work and behavior
- School Counselor—is asked about the student's overall progress in school, and whether there is a history of social or behavior problems
- Student—is asked what he thinks his problem is, what his thoughts and feelings are, why he thinks he acts the way he does at home and school
- Family doctor or pediatrician—is asked about the child's overall health, including vision and hearing, and whether there is a history of medical problems
- Child psychiatrist (doctor who works with children who have learning and behavioral problems) —may be asked to observe the child in both school and non-school settings and give an opinion on the child's actions
- Neurologist (doctor who works with the brain and physical disorders)—may be asked to observe the

One symptom of ADD is difficulty organizing and completing projects.

child in school and nonschool settings and give an opinion on physical mobility and coordination

# Diagnosis

When all the information from the tests, evaluations, and observations has been combined, a medical diagnosis is made. A diagnosis of ADD is given *only if the child has a lifelong history* of most of the following symptoms:

- being easily distracted
- difficulty paying attention
- difficulty listening
- difficulty organizing and completing tasks, projects, and activities
- avoidance of activities and tasks that require much effort
- tendency to lose things needed in daily activities
- tendency to forget things needed in daily activities

A diagnosis of ADHD is given *only if the child has a lifelong history* of most of the symptoms listed above, plus most of the following symptoms:

- constant fidgeting, squirming, running, or climbing
- inability to participate in quiet activities
- difficulty waiting in turn
- pushing, shoving, and intruding on others
- talking excessively

# What Diagnosis Means

If you are diagnosed with ADD or ADHD, you now

know that your problem is a real medical disorder. That lifts a huge load off your shoulders. And it means that you can start treatments and therapies that can help manage the disorder.

For parents of a child with ADD or ADHD, diagnosis means that their child is not suffering from " bad parenting." That lifts a great load off their shoulders, too. The diagnosis also lets them know that there are things *they* can do to help their child do better at home and at school.

For some parents, a diagnosis of ADD or ADHD also starts them thinking about their own childhood and some of the "problems" they had as they were growing up. After a diagnosis of ADD or ADHD has been made for their child, many parents say, "That sounds just like me when I was a kid."

For brothers, sisters, and classmates, a diagnosis of ADD or ADHD means there is a real reason—not just a bad attitude, laziness, or stupidity—for the way their sibling or friend acts. It also means that things will be less tense and stressful at home and at school once treatment is begun.

For teachers, a diagnosis of ADD or ADHD in a student means that classroom changes and accommodations (different strategies, techniques, and instructional practices) can be made to help the student become more successful in school.

Diagnosis is a win-win situation for everyone!

# Chapter 2

# Medication: The First Step

ADD and ADHD are medical disabilities, just as nearsightedness is. The medical treatment for nearsightedness is glasses. They don't "cure" the problem, but they do help bring the world into focus.

Treatment for ADD and ADHD can help bring the world into focus, too.

The treatment is multimodal. That means it uses a combination of things to help a person with ADD or ADHD to focus attention and concentration; to minimize impulsive and hyperactive behavior; and to deal with the emotional, social, behavioral, and educational problems that are symptoms of ADD and ADHD.

For most teens with ADD or ADHD, especially those with moderate or severe cases, treatment usually begins with medication. Two major classes of medication are used: stimulants and antidepressants.

Multimodal treatment helps people with ADD/ADHD deal with emotional problems.

After medication begins to take effect, multimodal treatment is expanded. Counseling and behavior modification are common components of multimodal treatment for a teen with ADD/ADHD.

## Medication: Pros and Cons

Medication will not cure ADD or ADHD, and it will not control emotional or behavioral problems. But it can improve your ability to concentrate and calm down. That makes it easier for you to work on the other problems that are part of the ADD/ADHD package: poor social skills, low grades, family problems, or low self-esteem.

Medications seem to work for more than 90 percent of people who try them. Though "meds" are a useful tool in the treatment of ADD/ADHD, there is still a lot of discussion about prescribing them.

The major concern of both parents and teens is that the medications used to treat ADD/ADHD are drugs. They worry that use of drugs for a medical disorder may lead to drug addiction. They also worry that too much medication may be prescribed by the doctor.

These are very real concerns. However, the drugs used to treat ADD and ADHD are not, in themselves, addictive. When they are prescribed by a doctor who knows a lot about ADD and ADHD, and are taken under the supervision of a responsible adult (such as a parent or school nurse), there is little chance that too much medication may be given or taken.

## Finding the Right Medication

"When a medication works, it works almost immediately. There are positive changes right off the bat," says Dr. Julie Wilson, a child psychologist at Brown University School of Medicine.

Of the stimulants, Ritalin, Dexedrine, and Cylert seem to be the medications that work the best for people with ADD or ADHD. Between 70 and 75 percent of people diagnosed with ADD or ADHD have success with these three medications.

In people who do not have ADD or ADHD, stimulants cause many of the symptoms of ADD and ADHD—hyperactivity, nervousness, inability to concentrate. Doctors do not fully understand why stimu-

Stimulants help improve many skills such as playing a musical instrument.

lants work differently for people with ADD and ADHD. However, they think stimulants help the brain "put on the brakes." When that happens, a person can calm down and focus attention.

The most common stimulants used to treat ADD/ADHD are Ritalin and Dexedrine. They are pills that begin working thirty to forty-five minutes after they are taken. Their effects last for three to four hours. That is why students who are using them need to take a "booster" pill at lunch time. It is also why they may need another pill if they are going to do an activity—a homework project, play in a basketball game—that requires focus and concentration in the evening.

The other common stimulant is Cylert. It acts more slowly than Dexedrine or Ritalin, but the effect usually lasts nine to twelve hours. That can be a definite plus in school, or on long car trips.

Stimulants do not work for everyone with ADD or ADHD. They may have little or no effect on concentration or hyperactive behavior. Or they may produce unpleasant side effects such as headaches or weight loss. In cases like these, some people take antidepressants, such as Tofranil, Norpramin, or Prozac.

When used to tread ADD/ADHD, antidepressants produce most of the same effects as stimulants. Some antidepressants also seem to help two other problems—bedwetting and sleepwalking—that often accompany ADD or ADHD.

## Medication Pros and Cons

The stimulants and antidepressants commonly used for ADD or ADHD have both pluses and minuses.

The pluses include:
• increased ability to concentrate and focus attention
• less overall restlessness and hyperactivity
• less impulsive behavior
• less aggressive behavior
• improved grades in school
• improved social interaction

The minuses include:
• appetite and weight loss
• inability to sleep through the night

Stimulants and antidepressants can help a person with ADD/ADHD improve his or her social interactions.

- headaches or stomachaches
- sleepiness
- sadness or irritability
- increased hyperactivity

## Is Medication Forever?

For many people with ADD or ADHD, medication is not a forever-after matter. Many doctors suggest "medication vacations," so teens often do not take medication after school, on weekends, during school vacations, or in the summertime. Also, some people with mild cases of ADD or ADHD seem to outgrow many of their symptoms—restlessness, talkativeness, lack of organization, poor grades, poor social skills—in their late teens. When that happens, they often discontinue taking medication.

In general, however, about half the people who take medication for ADD or ADHD continue taking it, either regularly or when they are involved in special projects, into adulthood.

# Chapter 3
# Counseling and Behavior Modification

W hen Robert started taking medication for his moderate ADHD, the family doctor suggested that he also see a counselor.

Boy, did that make him mad. He wasn't a mental case, and he wasn't a juvenile delinquent, either.

At first, he just sat in the counselor's office. He had to be there, but he didn't have to talk to her.

But the counselor always seemed to want to talk about things that were bothering Robert. During several sessions, they talked about how angry and hurt he was that no one even noticed how his grades had improved.

During other sessions, they talked about Robert's family, especially his "way-too-perfect" sister, Patricia. "She's such a nag," complained Robert.

The counselor suggested that he look at Patricia's nagging as coaching. "When she nags, try doing things

*her way," suggested the counselor. "At the very least,"
she added, "you'll quiet her down."*

*Robert tried the counselor's suggestion and was
amazed. "You know," he admitted to her, "when Pat's
nagging, she just wants me to do what's good for me. I
never looked at it that way."*

*Robert was in counseling for sixteen months. During
his last session, he thanked the counselor for what she'd
done.*

*She just laughed. "It wasn't me doing all the work,
Rob," she said. "It was you. I just listened."*

## What Is Counseling?

Counseling is nothing more than talking. But talking
puts your problems, fears, hopes, dreads, and dreams
into words.

For most teens with ADD or ADHD, counseling
(some people call it therapy) is a very important part
of managing their disability. It helps them uncover
their feelings of confusion, impatience, frustration,
anger, resentment, fear, hurt, shame, and guilt because
of their medical disability. It also helps them discover
strengths they didn't know they had—sensitivity to
others, creativity, high energy levels, enthusiasm, and
adaptability.

In counseling, you and the counselor sometimes play-
act family or school problems or social situations. When
you "act out" things that have been bugging and bothering you, you often find that they aren't as bad as you

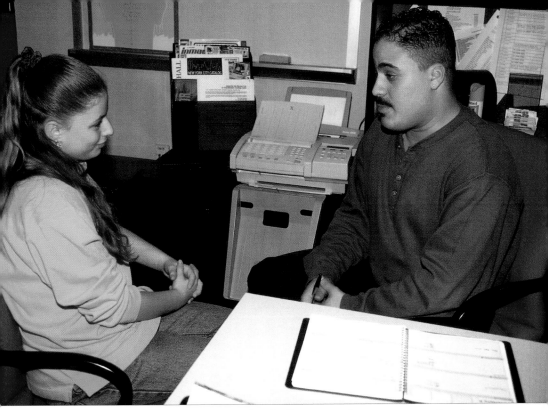
Counseling helps to uncover the feelings you have as a result of your medical disability.

thought. At other times you discover that problems really *are* as bad as they seem, but two heads—yours and the counselor's—can solve them more easily and faster.

Sometimes counseling is done in peer group sessions. In this kind of counseling, teens who share many of the same problems, or who have gone through many of the same situations, share solutions and insights on them.

At other times, counseling may include other family members. It is important for them to participate in counseling, too. Even though they do not have the disorder they are affected by it.

Counseling is an important part of treatment for ADD and ADHD because it allows you to blow off steam, helps you see problems as they really are, and

*25*

helps you solve them. But its most important functions are to "introduce" you to a new you and show you that it is possible to have a happy and successful life.

## What Is Behavior Modification?

*As Tyrone walked past Marc's desk to turn in his American History test, he knocked Marc's test to the floor.*

*"You spaz," Marc sputtered as he jumped to his feet. "I'm gonna…*

*Mr. Jackson walked quickly to Marc's desk. "Go put your test on my desk," he said to Tyrone. Then, in a voice pitched so low that Tyrone couldn't hear, he said, "Marc, take a deep breath and count to ten."*

*Marc took a gulp of air and held it for a moment, then he let it out slowly. "Naw," he said after a moment. "I'm okay. I don't need to count."*

*Marc bent down and picked up his test and slid back into his seat. In a few seconds he was hunched back over his test.*

*Mr. Jackson stood looking down at the top of Marc's head. He thought, why didn't someone teach Marc those behavior modification tricks years ago?*

In order to get the full benefits of a multimodal treatment plan, people with ADD or ADHD need to combine counseling with behavior changes. These changes replace the negative behaviors and attitudes that have built up over the years with positive ones.

Attitude and behavior changes, especially major ones, won't just happen on their own. They must be shoehorned into a person's daily life through the use of what psychologists call behavior modification therapy.

While counseling helps people get in touch with their thoughts and feelings, behavior modification helps them develop new (and better) behaviors to replace their old, self-sabotaging feelings, attitudes, and behaviors.

For example, when Marc took a "time-out" breather before he took a swing at Tyrone, he substituted positive behavior (thinking, calming himself) for a negative one (punching Tyrone's lights out).

Marc's new behavior allowed him to finish his test and go home at the end of the day feeling good about himself. If he had acted like the "old" Marc, he would have failed his test and been suspended. Again.

Think of behavior modification as "self-training." It helps a person with ADD/ADHD "do the right thing" in everyday situations and in situations that are new to him or her.

When you are learning behavior modification techniques, you usually have to stop and think about every little move you make. After a while, however, the new ways of thinking and feeling and acting become so natural that they kick in on their own.

## Find a Coach

While it is possible to change some behaviors on your own, it's easier and faster if you work with someone who can help you stick with the program. That means finding a personal "coach."

Peer group sessions enable teens to share their problems, solutions, and insights.

A coach isn't a substitute parent or a personal nag. He or she is someone who will:

- help you practice positive, new ways to deal with negative, old behaviors
- offer suggestions, advice, reminders, support, and (most important of all) encouragement
- help you get organized so you can set and reach goals
- help you recognize successes (and near-successes)
- help you deal with failures (and figure out why they occurred)

A coach should be someone that you like, but he or she should also be a "neutral" person. The best coaches are people who are firm and fair. They will be strict and tough on you if that is what is needed to keep you headed in the right direction.

Though parents, siblings, and friends should work with the coach, in most cases they do not make good coaches. Who then?

It definitely should be someone you respect and who cares about and respects you. That could be a teacher, a school guidance counselor, a therapist, or a close family friend. It could be an adult you know through your church or synagogue, or through community organizations such as the recreation center or "Y", Boys and Girls Clubs, Boy or Girl Scouts, Big Brothers/Big Sisters, or 4-H.

# Chapter 4

# Success Strategies at Home and School

*S*andy used to be disorganized and forgetful. At home she was constantly daydreaming or racing frantically through the house looking for shoes, the homework she'd spent an hour on the night before, her allowance money, the cordless phone, or her purse. Her parents constantly nagged about her room and chores. She made it to afterschool meetings or weekend parties only if friends called (and called and called) to remind her.

*At the end of her freshman year her severe ADD was diagnosed. She began taking Ritalin and got into a summertime counseling group at her school. There she learned strategies to use at home to help her manage her disorder.*

*At first Sandy didn't believe that talking and "little bits of paper" could help things at home. She soon found, however, that a wall calendar helped her remember appointments (and parties!); that using to-do lists helped her get all her chores done without the usual nagging from her parents; and that the notes she taped on her closet door, bedroom mirror, and the front door helped her remember to hang up her clothes and tell her parents where she was going when she left the house.*

*"I hated living with all those little yellow pieces of paper,"* Sandy said, *"but it sure beat the way things were before. Now,"* she added, *"I've gotten to the point where I remember things on my own—well, most of the time— before I see a note."*

# Improving Things on the Home Front

Learning coping strategies and techniques for the major symptoms of ADD and ADHD (forgetfulness, lack of organization, impulsiveness, and poor people skills) can turn things completely around at home. They make your home a lot less stressful because they add structure, order, and success to your life.

Learning home-front coping skills isn't something that can be done alone. To find successful ways to deal with the baggage that comes along with ADD or ADHD, you need to do some reading (see the For Further Reading section at the end of this book). You also need to work cooperatively with your parents and siblings, and you may need to work with a counselor or coach, too.

Keeping clothes together is one way to get organized.

Here are some techniques and strategies you can try now, however, that are guaranteed to turn things around at home.

<u>Get organized</u>. It is easier to keep track of things and keep organized if similar things are stored together. In the closet, shirts should go with shirts, pants with pants. In the dresser, have special drawers for underwear and sweaters. To add more storage space, put shelves into your closet and up on bedroom walls. Mark them with the names of the items that go on them.

<u>Make lists</u>. Once a day, or once a week, make a list of the activities and chores—ranked from most important to least important—that you need to do. Always check things off so you will see what you have accomplished.

Create routines. Do things that you have to do on a daily or weekly basis—take out the trash, deliver neighborhood newspapers, mow the lawn—at the same time, in the same way, every time you do them.

Keep a "my stuff" box at the foot of the stairs or near the front door. Put things you need to carry upstairs or take with you when you leave the house.

Learn to negotiate. If there are problems with family members, hold family meetings to to solve them. During these sessions, negotiate trade-offs (win-win situations) that solve the problems. For instance, get your parents to agree to let you have a swim party on the weekend (you win!) if you keep your room clean all week (they win!). Or get them to let you use the car for a Saturday night date (you win!) if you wash and wax it (they win!).

Exercise—running, roller blading, or other aerobic excercise will help you keep in shape and reduce stress. Exercise also releases a natural feel-good hormone, seratonin, into the body.

## Making School Work for You, Not Against You

*Reginald's severe ADHD was not diagnosed until near the end of the eighth grade, when he had a minor brush with the law. Medication helped him manage his disorder. His relationships with his family, teachers, and classmates improved dramatically. When he found out that poor grades would keep him from running track, he finally took an interest in his schoolwork.*

Making a list of things to do is one way to keep track of chores.

*He knew he was able to stay focused and pay attention much better in the morning, so when he started ninth grade he asked the counselor to reschedule his toughest classes for the morning. He also read a "study-smarter" book and asked the counselor for tips on how to better manage his classwork and homework.*

*The information helped, but Reginald still pulled an F in math and a D in Spanish the first marking period. Those kinds of grades would keep him off the track team in the spring, so he asked the counselor about tutoring. A phone call to the local community college got him into their Saturday morning program.*

*When spring track try-out time arrived, Reginald's grades weren't stellar—he had a D in math—but they didn't keep him off the team. And he didn't just make the team, he was elected co-captain.*

In most schools, every student is required to sit still at a desk, pay attention to the lessons and to the teacher, and cooperate with teachers, students, and "the system." These are the very things that a student with ADD or ADHD can't do.

This means that students with ADD and ADHD have major problems at school. It also means that a teacher is often the first one to suggest a test for ADD or ADHD.

Teachers can be your best allies if you have ADD or ADHD. Students with ADD or ADHD need their teachers' understanding, cooperation, and classroom accommodations in order to do their best.

# Tackling School Problems

If you have ADD or ADHD, it's a good idea to make an appointment with all your teachers at the beginning of each school year. Talk with them about your disability. With some teachers, you can make a "learning contract." This is an agreement listing the steps you are both going to take to help you succeed in class.

Here are some proven self-management, organizational, and study strategies that work for students and teachers. Use as many of them as you can.

Sit in the front of the class so you are not distracted by other students, and so the teacher can see when you do not understand something.

Organize notebooks and folders. Have separate, different colored folders for each class. Divide folders into three sections. Use the front section to record homework assignments, and check off when they are done. Use the middle section for notes and classwork. Use the last section to store returned homework and tests that you should review for final exams.

Take notes your way. When a class requires a lot of notes, write down important and/or key words, then borrow and photocopy a classmate's or the teacher's notes. In foreign language class, or in classes where there is a lot of information, use a tape recorder. Then listen to the tape at home and take notes at your own speed.

Ask for extra time on everything, especially tests. If possible, take tests orally. But make sure that when you set extended deadlines, you are able to meet them.

Get feedback. Ask the teacher for a checklist of your most common written mistakes. Use it to proofread homework, and if possible, the work done in class.

# Tips for Homework Success

Academic success isn't built only on what you do in the classroom. It's built on homework, too. There is a lot you can do at home to make sure that homework and special projects are done well and turned in on time.

Create a school calendar. Purchase a large wall calendar and enter on it all school-related activities—homework assignments, tests, special projects, contests, and programs. Use it to help you schedule study time for tests and pace yourself so you do not have several things due on the same day.

Have a special place for homework. Keep it stocked with school "tools"—pens, white-out, a dictionary, a calculator. If possible, keep copies of school textbooks here, too.

Manage your time. Do only one thing at a time, and pace work by breaking assignments down into smaller parts. For example, if you have a report due in two weeks, spend a couple of nights doing research, then schedule another couple of nights to organize information and outline the report. Give yourself a week to actually write the report. And finally, spend one evening, a couple of nights before it is due, proofreading it.

Use a kitchen timer or alarm clock to help you set and meet timed deadlines for completing homework assign-

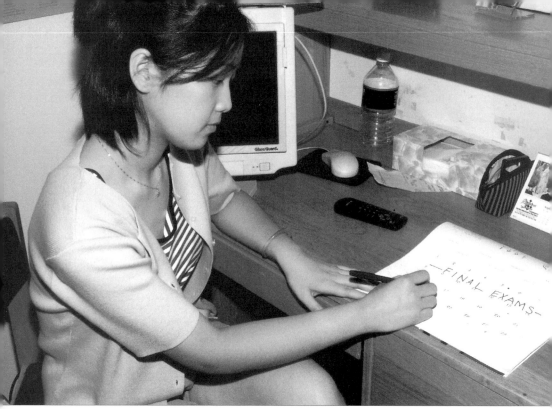

Writing events on a calendar can help you remember important appointments.

ments, or parts of them. When you have finished a timed assignment, take a break to give your brain a breather.

Use aids to help you remember things. Make and use flash cards for foreign language class. If you learn better when you hear things, read text assignments and notes into a tape recorder and play them back. When memorizing, turn information into silly sentences or words. For instance, HOMES isn't lots of houses, it's the Great Lakes (Huron, Ontario, Michigan, Erie, Superior).

Improve your proofreading skills. Always go over homework a second time. If possible, do all written work on a computer, then use punctuation, grammar, and spell-check functions to check your work. If you do not have a computer, read homework out loud or from the bottom up. Both systems help you catch errors.

# Your Legal Rights at School

ADD and ADHD interfere with the ability to learn and interact with others, so the United States Department of Education (DOE) considers them disabilities "which adversely affect...educational performance."

People with ADD and ADHD qualify for special, free services from their schools. This is guaranteed by two U.S. laws: the Individuals with Disabilities Education Act (Part B) and the Vocational Rehabilitation Act (Section 504). In most cases, these services include:

- Medical diagnosis, by the school system, of ADD or ADHD
- Creation of an individual educational program (IEP)—with input from school counselors, teachers, school administrators, and parents—to meet an ADD or ADHD student's unique educational needs
- Reasonable accommodations—such as seating changes, additional time for tests, or the substitution of oral for written work—to aid in educational performance

These services are usually available until a person reaches the age of twenty-one or leaves school, so they are available in college and technical school, too.

When schools are underfunded, overcrowded, or understaffed, or if the staff is overwhelmed with other responsibilities (or just won't cooperate), students with ADD or ADHD may have problems getting the special services to which they are entitled. That may mean that parents will have to become forceful spokespersons for their child. They may have to write detailed letters, make time-consuming calls, and/or visit their child's school on a regular basis.

Being their child's spokesperson may even mean that parents will have to take legal action against a school board. If that is necessary, parents should contact one of the ADD/ADHD support groups listed in this book. Or they should call the local office of the American Civil Liberties Union (see the white pages for a telephone number) for advice.

# Chapter 5

# Getting a Life (Back)

*Nilda's mother is a prize-winning artist. Her father is an internationally recognized chemist. Her sister is a staff writer for* Newsweek. *Her brother is at Harvard on a National Merit Scholarship.*

*Shy, dreamy, and disaster-prone, Nilda has always felt like the family failure. "I think there must have been a mix-up at the hospital," she once joked.*

*At the beginning of tenth grade, Nilda was diagnosed with a severe case of ADD. As soon as she began taking medication and working with a coach, her grades strated inching upward. The number of accidents she was involved in began to drop. Her circle of friends began to grow.*

*At the end of the school year, however, Nilda had not noticed any of these changes. She was still convinced that she was dumb, disorganized, and klutzy.*

Nilda's situation is very common. Many people whose ADD or ADHD is not recognized until they are in their late teens have already lost much self-esteem. Their undiagnosed disorder has already caused them frustration, anxiety, anger, and embarrassment. It got them teased, picked on, nagged, and grounded. It contributed to many of their failures—flunked tests, failed friendships, flubbed driver's license tests. It also caused them many personal problems with their family, friends, and teachers. It may even have got them into trouble with the law.

It *is* possible to rebuild self-confidence, self-esteem, and feelings of self-worth after a diagnosis of ADD or ADHD. And it is easier than you think. But rebuilding takes time, effort, and confidence that change is possible.

Rebuilding self-esteem and self-confidence does not mean getting back at people or becoming a superteen. It *does* mean seeing the positives that ADD or ADHD carry with them, and discovering the real you.

## Recognize Strengths

If you have ADD or ADHD, you know all about the problems it causes. However, many of these "problems" have a flip side. Those flip sides carry some wonderful hidden strengths.

For instance, inability to focus on one thing at a time becomes a strength if it is turned into an ability to adjust to constantly changing situations. A constant need to be on the go is a strength when it is funneled

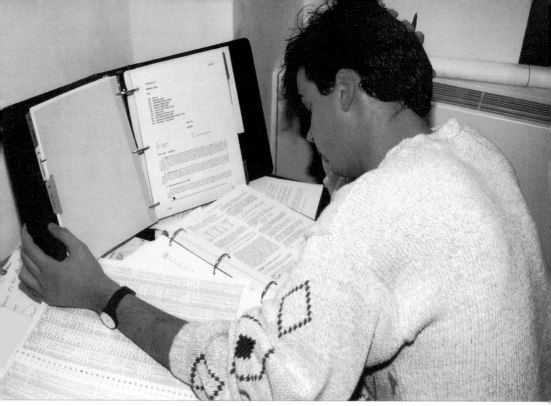

The more you know about ADD/ADHD, the more confident you will become.

into sports, scientific research, or other high-focus/high-energy activities. Daydreaming is a strength when employed in artistic or creative situations.

Here is a list of some of the "negatives" that are often part of the ADD or ADHD package, and their flip sides.

- Slow worker (detail-oriented, careful, very observant)
- Withdrawn (deep or careful thinker, critical-minded)
- Judgmental (committed to fairness and justice)
- Easily hurt (attuned to others feelings and needs)
- Impatient (solution seeker, problem solver)
- Nonvisual learner (able to learn through other senses)

Joining an afterschool activity is one way to get your life back.

# Tips for Building Self-esteem and Self-confidence

To help you rebuild feelings of self-confidence and personal satisfaction, and discover the person who is buried under the baggage that comes with ADD or ADHD:

Educate yourself about your ADD or ADHD. Knowledge is power. The more you know about your medical disability, and how to manage its symptoms, the more confident you can become.

Psych yourself up for a new you. Use mental imaging to paint a picture of a new you—having better relationships with family members, making better grades, working at a part-time job. The more detailed the images, the more they will help you achieve the changes you want in your life.

Set reasonable goals. It's good to have goals and dreams. But be sure to set realistic ones.

Give yourself constructive criticism. When you don't achieve a goal, don't beat yourself up. Look closely at why you failed—poor organization, aiming too high, not enough hard work—and use failure as a teaching experience. Knowing what you did wrong will not turn a current mess into a success, but it will show you what not to do next time.

Join a peer support group. Participating in a peer group gives you a lot of insight into how bad your problems really are, and it also gives you tips on how to deal with some of the personal baggage you are carrying.

Additionally, it lets you practice social skills, such as how to keep your cool when someone bothers you, or how to solve problems that may come up with friends.

Join "fun" groups. Clubs and groups are peer support groups, but they are fun. At school, the debate or drama club may be a trial if you are shy, but the journalism club, chess club, or drill team won't be. If you like to help others, the volunteer organizations in your community or at museums, senior centers, or hospitals will put you in situations where you will be caring and sharing.

Take up a sport or hobby. The exercise you get in sports, even solo sports like golf, karate, or swimming, helps work off pent-up energy. The concentration you put into hobbies such as sewing, building spaceship models, or drawing and sketching does the same thing, but for your mind.

*Carol had an easier time reading after she started medication and counseling to manage her ADD. And as Carol was able to concentrate on reading, she became inspired to write her own stories. Sometimes she would pick up the characters from one story and continue them in the next one.*

*At first Carol didn't show her stories to anyone—she stockpiled them in her desk drawer for months. She was embarrassed about them, and thought that they probably weren't any good. But when her English teacher assigned a creative writing project, Carol sat down and let her imagination play with the characters and words again. She stopped writing after three pages, satisfied that she would continue the storyline later, and shyly turned in the story at the end of class.*

*Two days later her teacher, Mrs. Ramirez, pulled Carol aside. "I have to tell you how much I loved your story," she said. "You have to keep writing and let me know what happens! And I'd love to read more of your work, if you like. You have real talent."*

*Carol was shocked—no one had ever encouraged her so strongly before. Mrs. Ramirez was shocked because Carol had always been quiet, and had daydreamed through class. Mrs. Ramirez had had no idea that underneath the symptoms of ADD, Carol was a budding young writer.*

*Carol pulled out her old stories and gave them to Mrs. Ramirez to read. Mrs. Ramirez gave her feedback, and encouraged her to publish in the school literary magazine. Carol did more than that—she sent them to a teen magazine, and was published across the country.*

As self-esteem, self-confidence, and feelings of self-worth grow, they feed off each other. Strength leads to strength. As you become more sure of yourself, you become less angry, anxious, and reactive about your ADD or ADHD, and more proactive about yourself.

# Chapter 6

# Career Choices

*S*hane *was relieved when he was diagnosed with ADHD. It seemed as if people—his parents, teachers, and primary care doctor—were finally taking an interest in him. He no longer was written off as a troublemaker. His sister showed (just a little) more patience with him.*

*But Shane was also confused. When everyone thought he was a troublemaker, it was easy to give up on school-work. Now, as Shane slowly began to understand his disorder, he saw that he was going to work harder than he ever had before.*

*Shane talked with his counselor about his fears. The counselor said that Shane's fears were normal. And slowly, Shane began to realize that there is an up side to the new responsibilities he faced: he could start aiming his thoughts and talents toward the future in a way he never could before.*

If you have been diagnosed with ADD or ADHD, you now have a name and (more important) a diagnosis and treatment plan for the problem that has been running your life. But it also creates questions of who you are and who you want to become.

## Just Like People without ADD or ADHD

People with ADD and ADHD have a wide variety of intellectual abilities, special talents, and unique interests—just like people without ADD or ADHD.

People with ADD or ADHD have personalities that range from life of the party to wallflower—just like people without ADD or ADHD.

People with ADD or ADHD range from being workaholics to slackers—just like people without ADD or ADHD.

And although ADD and ADHD are medical disabilities, when they are managed they are definitely not a handicap in the career world.

That means that when you are planning a career, you bring the same abilities, aptitudes, characteristics, and capabilities to a job search (and want the same things out of a job) as someone who doesn't have ADD or ADHD.

## Yes, You Need More Schooling After School

Most well-paying jobs require post-high school training at a technical school, junior college, or four-year college.

People with ADD/ADHD may become successful in an occupation such as computer programming.

So you should definitely consider more education after high school.

That's not as difficult as you may think.

Many schools have programs and curriculums that can meet the special needs of people with ADD or ADHD. In fact, technical schools and the technical programs at two-year colleges, with their shorter programs and hands-on learning, have always offered very good learning environments to people with ADD or ADHD. Some four-year colleges also have programs that are set up to meet the needs of, and guarantee success for, people with ADD or ADHD.

When you begin looking at post-high school career options, keep two things in mind:

- The career you choose should give you a chance to minimize your weaknesses and maximize your strengths, especially your unique ability to look at situations creatively and tap into very high energy levels.
- With or without post-high school training, people with ADD or ADHD usually have only limited success in careers that require lots of hands-on paperwork. For that reason, careers that require a lot of record-keeping, or highly detailed documentation—such as travel agent, executive secretary, or tax accountant—probably are not good choices.

# Good Career Choices

*While she never seemed to get things right at school and often left her chores undone, Sharon definitely had a healing touch. She played nurse to so many of the animals on her family's farm in Oklahoma, her brother referred to her room as "General Hospital."*

*It wasn't until high school that Sharon was diagnosed with ADD. With medication, better organization and time management techniques, and tutoring, Sharon finally began doing well in school—well enough, in fact, to be accepted to nursing school.*

*School wasn't easy. In order to keep her grades up and fit extra tutoring into her schedule, Sharon carried a lighter-than-normal class load. She also took a part-time job as an aide at a children's hospital. For those reasons, it took her five and a half years to complete a four-year program.*

*Sharon's perseverance, hard work, and maturity paid off. She was hired as a pediatric nurse by the first nursing supervisor who interviewed her.*

*Today, at twenty-nine, Sharon is back in school. She's training to become a pediatric surgical nurse.*

*Antonio's poor grades and quick temper didn't make him popular at school with classmates or teachers. But he was diagnosed with ADHD only after he had failed eighth grade.*

*Medication helped put the brakes on Antonio's hyperactivity and moodiness. And in ninth grade Antonio actually got interested in school. Computers were fun— they worked at his speed, not the teacher's, and Antonio began coming into the computer lab after work to do homework and reports.*

*In tenth grade, on the computer teacher's recommendation, Antonio began helping the journalism teacher lay out the school paper electronically. Using an old graphics program, he started drawing a cartoon strip for the paper.*

*Now, at twenty-two, Antonio is working at a Los Angeles studio that is famous for its state-of-the-art animated cartoons.*

When people with ADD have learned to use special organization and time management techniques, they are often successful as hotel, resort, or restaurant managers; police officers or private detectives; freelance writers or newspaper reporters; computer operators or programmers; building contractors or construction project managers; scientific researchers; corporate lawyers; and business and educational consultants.

Because people with ADD often tend to be empathetic (to see and understand the feelings and needs of others), they also do very well in the caring professions where they make excellent customer service representatives, airline attendants, social workers, hospice nurses, and teachers.

People with ADHD tend to be outgoing, high-energy, action-seeking people. Since they like excitement and new things, many choose careers that give them lots of freedom to move around at work or to travel, experience new situations, and interact with a variety of people. That is why many become very successful actors or musicians, professional athletes, trial lawyers, and politicians.

People with ADHD also are successful in careers that require a lot of instantaneous decision making, crisis management, or troubleshooting, such as emergency room doctor or nurse; Emergency Medical Services (EMS) or emergency repair technician; commercial airline pilot; or radio announcer or disk jockey.

Not surprisingly, since they are always seeing things in new ways, people with ADHD are successful as fiction writers, fashion and industrial designers, marketing and public relations specialists, salespeople, and motivational speakers. And because they are able to process many things at once, many people with ADHD become artists or inventors.

## Looking Ahead

With hard work and support, you will be able not only to " just get by" through school, but to follow your dreams wherever they lead you. You may find that what you *thought* were your ADD or ADHD's "negatives" will, in the long run, help you become the best person you can be.

# Glossary

**antidepressant** Prescription drug (medication) used to treat ADD/ADHD when stimulants do not work.

**attention deficit disorder (ADD)** A mild to severe medical disorder that is characterized by the inability to focus, concentrate, and pay attention for long periods of time.

**attention deficit hyperactivity disorder (ADHD)** attention deficit disorder (see above) accompanied by impulsivity and overactivity.

**behavior modification** Skills, strategies, and techniques that help change and modify the negative behaviors and attitudes that often accompany ADD or ADHD.

**counselor** A professional who works with people to help them understand their feelings and solve their problems.

**diagnosis** Identification and description of a medical condition or problem.

**distractable** Tendency to become easily distracted.

**empathetic** To be tuned in to and responsive to the feelings of others.

**extrovert** Person who has a very "up," outgoing personality.

**family counseling** Therapy or counseling sessions that involve the whole family.

**hyperactivity** Excessively active, restless, and impulsive behavior.

**impulsive** Acting or speaking without thinking or considering consequences.

**inattentive** Easily distracted, unable to pay attention.

**introvert** Person who is shy, reserved, or inward looking.

**low self-esteem** Lack of confidence or faith in one's capabilities.

**medication** Medicine used to treat illness or improve functioning of the brain or body.

**multimodal treatment** Treatment of a medical disorder that uses more than one method, program, or approach at the same time.

**neurotransmitter** Chemical substance produced by the body that acts as a messenger or signal carrier.

**peer group** People, usually of the same age and grade, who have many things in common.

**peer support group** A group of people with many of the same problems or goals who share information, insights, and feelings in a group setting.

**prioritize** To organize and rank tasks, problems, or projects according to their importance.

**sabotage** An act that is designed to slow or stop progress.

**self-confidence** Trust or faith in oneself and one's abilities.

**self-esteem** Feelings of confidence and personal worth.

**sibling** A brother or sister.

**stimulant** A medication or drug that increases energy and mental activity.

**strategy** A well-thought-out method or plan to achieve a goal.

**symptom** Characteristic or condition that results from or accompanies a disease or disorder. Symptoms help to diagnose many diseases and illnesses.

**therapist** Person—counselor, social worker, psychologist, or psychiatrist—who is specially trained to treat a disease or physical or mental condition.

**therapy** Treatment of disease or a mental disorder.

# Where to Go for Help

These agencies and organizations can supply you with more information on attention deficit disorder and attention deficit hyperactivity disorder and put you in touch with ADD/ADHD support groups in your area.

ADD Warehouse (catalog and supplies)
300 Northwest 70th Avenue, Suite 102
Plantation, FL 33317
(800) 233-9273
web site: www.addwarehouse.com

Children and Adults with Attention Deficit Disorder
    (CHAAD)
499 Northwest 70th Avenue
Plantation, FL 33317
(800) 233-4050; (954) 587-3700
web site: www.chadd.org

Learning Disabilities Association of America (LDA)
4156 Library Road
Pittsburgh, PA 15234
(412) 341-1515; (412) 341-8077
web site: www.ldanatl.org
e-mail: ldanatl@usaor.net

National Attention Deficit Disorder Association (ADDA)
9930 Johnnycake Ridge Road  #3-E
Mentor, Ohio  44060

Tel: (800) 487-2282 or (216) 350-9595
web site: www.add.org
e-mail: natladda@aol.com

National Center for Learning Disabilities (NCLD)
381 Park Avenue South
Suite 1401
New York, NY  10016
Tel: (212) 545-7510
web site: www.ncld.org
e-mail: ncld@paltech.com

National Information Center for Children and Youth with
    Disabilities (NICHCY)
Box 1492
Washington, DC  20013-1492
(800) 695-0285
web site: http://www.nichcy.org

# In Canada

CHAAD Canada
1376 Bank Street
Ottawa, Ontario  K1H 1B2
(613) 731-1207

Learning Disabilities Association of Canada
323 Chapel Street, Suite # 200
Ottawa, Ontario  KIN 7Z2
(613) 238-5721

Self-Help Resource Center of Greater Toronto
40 Orchard View Blvd., Suite #219
Toronto, Ontario  M4R 1B9
(416) 487-4355
e-mail: shrc@inforamp.net

# Online Information
There are several on-line bulletin boards where parents, teens, adults with ADD or ADHD, and medical professionals share experiences, offer emotional support, and ask and answer ADD/ADHD-related questions.

CompuServe USA and Canada:     (800) 848-8990
Outside USA and Canada:        (614) 457-0802
America Online:                (800) 827-6364
Prodigy:                       (800) 776-3449

Americans with Disabilities Act (ADA) and/or Disability Information
http://www.public.iastate.edu/~sbilling/ada.html

Attention Deficit Disorder Archives
http://homepage.seas.upenn.edu/~mengwong/add/

One ADD Place
http://www.greatconnect.com/oneaddplace/

# For Further Reading

**For Teens**

Ignoffo, Matthew. *Everything You Need to Know about Self-confidence*. New York: Rosen Publishing Group, 1996.

James, Elizabeth, and Barkin, Carol. H*ow to Be School Smart: Secrets of Successful Schoolwork*. New York: Lothrop, Lee & Shepard Books, 1988.

Kaufman, Gershen, and Raphael, Lev. *Stick Up for Yourself!: Every Kid's Guide to Personal Power and Positive Self-Esteem*. Minneapolis, MN: Free Spirit Publishing, 1990.

Morris, Jaydeen. *Coping with ADD/ADHD*. New York: Rosen Publishing Group, 1996.

Quinn, Patricia. *Adolescents and ADD: Gaining the Advantage*. New York: Magination Press, 1995.

Wirths, Claudine, and Bowman-Kruhm, Mary. *I Hate School: How to Hang In & When to Drop Out*. New York: Harper & Row, 1987.

**For Parents**

Dendy, Chris. T*eenagers with ADD: A Parents Guide*. Bethesda, MD: Woodbine House, 1995.

Hartman, Thom. *Think Fast!: The ADD Experience.*
Grass Valley, CA: Underwood Books, 1995.
(Includes the best resource section I encountered!)

Pierangelo, R. and Jacoby, R. *Parents' Complete Special Guide: Tips, Techniques, & Materials for Helping Your Child Succeed in School and Life.* New York: Center for Applied Research in Education, 1996.

Weiss, Lynn, Ph.D. *Give Your ADD Teen a Chance: A Guide for Parents of Teenagers with Attention Deficit Disorder.* Colorado Springs, CO: Pinon Press, 1996.

**For Teachers and Counselors**

Mangrum, Charles and Strichart, Stephen. *Peterson's Guide to Colleges with Programs for Students with Learning Disabilities.* Princeton, NJ: Petersons Guides, 1998.

Parker, Harvey. *The ADD Hyperactivity Handbook for Schools.* Plantation, FL: Impact Publications, 1992.

Rief, Sandra. *How to Reach and Teach ADD/ADHD Children.* New York: Center for Applied Research in Education, 1993.

# Index

## About the Author

Eileen Beal has an M.A. in history and museum education. She has worked as a junior and senior high school social studies teacher, an assistant editor for both magazines and newspapers, a free-lance food and restaurant critic, and a free-lance writer. She is the author of *Choosing a Career in the Restaurant Industry*, also by Rosen Publishing.

## Photo Credits

Photo on p. 11 by Skjold Photography; p. 43 by Ira Fox; all other photos and cover by Ethan Zindler